Find Your

Profitable Niche

Identify Your Domain, Fuel Your Passion, Create Value for Your Audience and Design Your Successful Career Path

Clear Career Inclusive

Want to get our book for free?

Discover the 16 different personality types with MBTI. Each of us has unique talents that make our personality shine. Want to dive into the deeper psychology of your type, explore your special cognitive functions, and find your path to personal growth? Scan the QR code below to grab your free copy of the Personality Handbook now.

Contents

About the Series

Who has time for long books or endless coaching sessions in our fast-paced world? With the proper guidance, though, you can make more intelligent, more impactful decisions. This series offers powerful insights and practical tips in quick, easy-to-read formats, helping you take control of your career without draining your time. We encourage you to dive deeper into areas that resonate with you before deciding and finding what truly fits your path.

Design Your Successful Career Path

- Book 1: _Raise Your Income Potential_
- Book 2: _Find Your Profitable Niche_
- Book 3: _Build Your Personal Brand_

About the Book

Many of us enter a job or select a course of study based on the opportunities available, our academic grades, financial situation, or aspirations. Only a few choose their career paths purely out of personal interest. However, your career isn't limited to the jobs you undertake; it's also about the value you add to your work and the extent you excel in it, even if you're not employed traditionally.

This book offers insights on identifying the areas of least resistance on your path to success. This route with the least effort allows you to develop a long-term, fulfilling career.

Key takeaways from this book include how to:

1. Discover niche opportunities
2. Stand out in your niche
3. Create value for your audience

Since our mental and physical energy is subject to depletion, it will be wise to focus it on specific areas with an excellent chance of succeeding.

Introduction

Our environment shapes us. From the moment we are born, we don't choose our family or the society we're a part of. Our early lives are primarily influenced by the people closest to us, and over time, we develop a personality that helps us survive and thrive in that environment.

But real growth comes when we step outside our familiar surroundings—whether for work, study, or new experiences. We adapt, acquire new skills, and continue to evolve. Each new environment adds layers to our development, but it's essential to recognize that our exposure remains limited. This is where the concept of integrated development becomes a game-changer, empowering us to take control of our growth: the understanding that to truly grow, we must seek out what's missing and consciously develop those areas.

Integrated development rarely happens by chance. It often requires deliberate effort, similar to students attending coaching classes to achieve specific results. Success doesn't come from just going through the motions; it's a system that demands dedication and focus. Similarly, developing our personality to its fullest potential requires learning—whether through self-reflection or external guidance.

One obstacle that often stands in the way of growth is the ego. The ego tells us we've already learned enough and don't need to change. But growth requires adaptability. We must accept that we will not be able to master every skill or subject, and that's why finding a niche becomes essential. Instead of spreading ourselves too thin, it would be wise to focus on a specific area where our natural strengths lie.

Psychologists like Carl Jung have long studied the patterns of personality development, showing that people thrive when they work within their cognitive strengths. By focusing on a niche that aligns with your personality and strengths, you're not only more likely to succeed but will find that learning and growth come more naturally.

But it's not enough to simply identify a niche—you also need an audience. A profitable niche is one where there's a clear demand for your services and where people are willing to invest in what you offer. In this book, we'll explore how to discover niche opportunities, stand out from the crowd, and create value for your audience to sustain long-term growth in your chosen niche.

Greg Norman once said, 'Know your strengths and take advantage of them.' In the book *Raise Your Income Potential*, we discussed how to identify your strengths. In this book, we will dive deeper into how you can take full advantage of those strengths to align with a profitable niche.

You may be a student, a professional, or already running a business. The purpose of this book is to help you align better with a profitable niche that leverages your unique personality strengths. Your niche is similar to your *ikigai*—a purpose in life that aligns you toward success with minimal effort.

1. Discover Niche Opportunities

"One of the outstanding tragedies of this age of struggle and money madness is the fact that so few people are engaged in the effort which they like best. Everyone should find his or her particular niche in the world's work, where both material prosperity and happiness in abundance may be found."- **Napoleon Hill.**

Many thought leaders speak about investing in your strengths and following your passion, but how do we truly implement that? For most people, the journey starts by following a well-trodden path— pursuing a degree that leads to a stable job or opting for a career based solely on financial security. Yet, despite financial success, many still feel unfulfilled, proving that money alone does not define success.

But what if there's a niche where you can excel, one you still need to discover? An area that not only brings in income but satisfies your inner calling and allows you to serve others? Imagine how far you could go doing something that excites you rather than that which drains you.

"People rarely succeed unless they have fun in what they are doing." - **Dale Carnegie.**

What is a Niche?

The Cambridge Dictionary defines a niche as "a job or position very suitable for someone, especially one they like." It's a space where you harness your strengths and interests to meet a demand for which people are willing to pay. Niches can be defined by price, demographics, quality, psychographics, geography, lifestyle, profession, culture, habits, or other specific traits and can evolve into different niches over time.

A niche market strategy combines strong market demand, addressing a practical need, high profit potential, minimal competition, and personal fulfillment. Sustaining your niche is about aligning your Ikigai—your reason for being—while refining your service and optimizing your offerings for profitability.

Why Should You Find Your Niche?

A balanced life is one where you enjoy what you do, use your skills to meet others' needs, and earn money. This is often described as successful intelligence—a blend of creative, analytical, and practical thinking. Finding your niche may sometimes conflict with the extrinsic motivators of the job market, like making the most money from any available opportunity. However, it also deeply honors your intrinsic motivators—strengths, passions, and desires.

No one will push you toward your niche; you must actively seek it. Finding your niche doesn't necessarily mean you'll always stay within your comfort zone. Like any business, you may need to adapt and upskill, but your strengths will allow you to overcome challenges easily. When you find the right audience who are willing to pay for what you love to do, you set yourself on a path toward long-term success.

"A man's true delight is to do the things he was made for." – **Marcus Aurelius.**

This idea aligns with the Japanese concept of Ikigai and the law of Dharma, both of which emphasize discovering your unique strengths to serve humanity. You're more likely to stay committed to something if you feel a natural pull toward it, which is critical if you're a freelancer or solopreneur.

Finding your niche is critical whether you're starting a blog, offering courses, or launching a startup. It's the foundation for building your brand and establishing long-term success.

"The best jobs are neither decreed nor degreed. They are creative expressions of continuous learners in free markets."- **Naval Ravikanth.**

Niche Opportunities in Freelancing

Freelancing offers immense opportunities for professionals passionate about working independently. However, passion alone is not enough to sustain a thriving freelance career. To maximize success, freelancers must align their interests and skills with niches that are in high demand. As businesses increasingly seek specialized expertise, choosing a niche offering substantial opportunities is crucial. Here are the most promising freelance niches based on industry trends and emerging market demands:

1. Digital Marketing

The digital marketing landscape continues to grow, with freelancers needed to help businesses reach online audiences. In-demand sub-niches include:

- SEO copywriting
- Social media marketing
- Email campaigns
- E-commerce content creation
- Pay-per-click (PPC) advertising
- Affiliate marketing
- Influencer marketing

- Content strategy consulting
- Video ad creation
- Marketing automation
- Online reputation management

Digital marketing involves crafting engaging content to build brand awareness and generate leads. Freelancers in this niche must keep up with industry trends, sharpen their persuasive writing skills, and master digital marketing tools.

2. Ghost writing

Ghost writing provides opportunities to write books, blogs, or speeches for others without receiving public credit. It's ideal for those who enjoy long-form narrative content, both fiction and non-fiction. This niche is gaining traction, especially in business, personal development, and content marketing. Sub-niches include:

- Business books
- Memoirs
- Thought leadership articles

- Speechwriting
- White papers
- Blog posts for niche markets (e.g., finance, health)
- Scriptwriting for podcasts or videos

3. Cryptocurrency and Blockchain

As blockchain technology expands, a demand for freelancers skilled in cryptocurrency content creation is growing. Writing in this niche requires knowledge of blockchain platforms, smart contracts, and the regulatory environment. Freelancers can produce content ranging from beginner-friendly guides to technical documents for seasoned investors. Sub-niches include:

- White papers on blockchain use cases
- NFT content development
- De Fi (Decentralized Finance) articles
- Crypto compliance writing
- Smart contract documentation

4. Healthcare

Healthcare content is among the highest-paying freelance niches due to its complexity and specialized knowledge requirements. Professionals with a background in medicine or healthcare writing are in demand to create educational guides, medical journal articles, and clinical reports. Sub-niches include:

- Medical blogging
- Healthcare technology writing
- Pharmaceutical copywriting
- Mental health content creation
- Fitness and wellness articles
- Patient education materials

5. Personal Finance

The evergreen personal finance niche provides valuable insights on money management, investment strategies, and credit monitoring. Freelancers in this niche help businesses produce content that guides consumers through financial literacy, savings plans, and long-term wealth-building techniques. Sub-niches include:

- Retirement planning guides
- Tax strategy content
- Personal investment newsletters
- Credit repair advice
- Cryptocurrency tax implications

6. Real Estate

Real estate companies leverage content marketing to attract clients and promote their services. Freelancers can find opportunities to write blog posts, email newsletters, home listings, and rental agreements. This niche offers consistent work in a growing market. Sub-niches include:

- Real estate photography
- Rental property management guides
- Real estate investing newsletters
- Virtual property tours
- Home staging advice

7. Technical Writing

Technical writing remains a lucrative niche for freelancers who can simplify complex subjects. This diverse niche covers business plans, white papers, user manuals, and SaaS content. Writers must have strong research skills and the ability to convey technical information. Sub-niches include:

- Software documentation
- API (Application Programming Interface) writing
- User experience research documentation
- IT security protocols
- Robotics manuals
- Telecommunications writing

8. Software-as-a-Service (SaaS)

SaaS is a booming field with constant demand for content writers who can craft persuasive and lead-driven blog posts. The competition is stiff, but opportunities abound for those with experience in tech writing. Sub-niches include:

- SaaS product launch content

- Customer success guides
- SaaS comparison articles
- Case studies for SaaS solutions

9. E-Learning and Online Courses

The e-learning sector has increased, creating opportunities for freelancers to produce course modules, scripts, and educational content. Freelancers with an education or curriculum development background can excel in this niche. Sub-niches include:

- Educational course creation for corporate training
- Gamification in e-learning
- Compliance training materials
- Interactive quiz development
- Microlearning modules

10. Website Development

Web development is a fast-growing career field for freelancers with coding, markup, and content management skills. Proficiency in JavaScript, Python, and HTML is in high demand. Freelancers can thrive in web design, front- and back-end development, and user experience (UX) design. Sub-niches include:

- WordPress development
- Shopify and e-commerce platforms
- Web accessibility consulting
- Progressive web app (PWA) development
- SEO-optimized web design

11. UI and UX Design

UI and UX designers ensure websites provide an intuitive and seamless user experience. Freelancers specializing in UI/UX design are in high demand for their ability to craft visually compelling and user-friendly digital interfaces. Sub-niches include:

- Mobile-first web design
- UX writing
- Prototyping and wireframing
- Usability testing
- Motion graphics design

12. Data Analytics

As more businesses rely on data-driven strategies, freelancers skilled in data analytics are highly sought after. Data analytics involves analyzing raw data to optimize business decisions. Freelancers in this niche can provide services in predictive analytics, prescriptive strategies, and data visualization. Sub-niches include:

- Marketing Analytics
- Financial forecasting
- Data visualization for executive presentations
- Sentiment analysis
- Customer behavior analysis

13. Social Media Management

While many freelancers provide social media content creation, social media management requires a more holistic approach. This niche involves handling content distribution, engaging with audiences, and creating strategies to grow a brand's online presence. Sub-niches include:

- Instagram growth strategies
- LinkedIn thought leadership
- YouTube video management
- Influencer collaborations
- Social media crisis management

14. Mobile App Development

Mobile app development is experiencing explosive growth, driven by increased mobile device usage. Freelancers with Swift, Java, C#, and HTML5 skills will find ample opportunities to build apps for various platforms, including e-commerce, entertainment, and education. Sub-niches include:

- Gaming app development
- Augmented reality (AR) apps
- App maintenance services
- FinTech mobile app development
- App Store Optimization (ASO)

15. Blockchain Development

With the rapid adoption of blockchain technologies, there is a high demand for developers specializing in building decentralized applications (DApps), token development, and smart contracts. Freelancers in this niche can work on emerging projects across industries. Sub-niches include:

- Decentralized app (DApp) development
- NFT marketplace creation
- Blockchain architecture consulting
- Tokenomics development
- Blockchain security auditing

16. Virtual Assistance

Virtual assistants (VAs) are essential for businesses looking to outsource administrative tasks and free up time for high-priority work. Freelancers can assist with various services, from customer service to specialized support. Sub-niches include:

- Podcast management
- E-commerce store support
- Event planning and coordination
- CRM management
- Email marketing automation

17. E-commerce Management

With online shopping growing exponentially, freelancers specializing in e-commerce management help businesses streamline their operations. Whether setting up stores or managing inventory, this niche offers opportunities to support the booming e-commerce sector. Sub-niches include:

- Inventory management systems
- Customer support via live chat
- Dropshipping store management
- Subscription box service setup
- Affiliate store management

18. Video Marketing

Video marketing continues to dominate the digital landscape, with businesses needing high-quality content for promotional purposes. Freelancers can specialize in creating various types of videos that drive engagement and sales. Sub-niches include:

- Tutorial video creation

- Video testimonials
- Event highlight reels
- Video SEO optimization
- Animated explainer videos

19. Artificial Intelligence (AI)

Freelancers with expertise in AI can help companies implement cutting-edge solutions, such as chatbots, machine learning algorithms, and automation systems. This niche is rapidly expanding, focusing on providing businesses with tools for more intelligent decision-making. Sub-niches include:

- AI chatbot development
- AI-driven marketing content
- Natural language processing models
- AI ethics consulting
- AI integration into apps

20. Cybersecurity

Cybersecurity is critical for businesses, especially with the rise of remote work and cloud services. Freelancers specializing in cybersecurity offer solutions to protect data, mitigate risks, and ensure regulatory compliance. Sub-niches include:

- Threat detection and mitigation strategies
- Cybersecurity compliance (e.g., GDPR, HIPAA)
- Data breach response planning
- Encryption consulting
- Cloud security solutions

21. Language Translation

As businesses expand globally, the need for high-quality translation services grows. Freelancers specializing in translating content for different markets can focus on localization, technical translation, and more. Sub-niches include:

- Localization of video games
- Legal document translation
- Technical manuals in multiple languages
- Live interpreting services
- Multilingual customer support

22. Sustainability Consulting

As businesses increasingly prioritize sustainability, freelancers in this niche can help organizations navigate environmental challenges and implement sustainable practices. This niche is vital for addressing climate change and promoting renewable energy solutions. Sub-niches include:

- Climate change consulting
- Renewable energy content development
- Sustainability reporting and assessment
- Corporate social responsibility (CSR) strategy

23. Fitness Training

The demand for online fitness solutions has surged, creating opportunities for freelancers to provide fitness coaching and wellness advice. This niche caters to individuals seeking healthier lifestyles through various platforms. Sub-niches include:

- Online fitness coaching
- Wellness blogging
- Nutrition planning
- Fitness program development

24. Podcast Production

The podcasting industry is booming, and freelancers can specialize in various aspects of podcast production, from editing to marketing. Sub-niches include:

- Podcast editing and production
- Audio branding and sound design
- Podcast marketing strategy
- Podcast transcription services
- Show notes and content creation

25. Fashion and Lifestyle

Freelancers can leverage their creativity and knowledge of trends to offer styling advice. Sub-niches include:

- Personal styling services
- Sustainable fashion content creation
- Fashion blogging and influencer marketing
- Fashion photography and videography

26. Photography

Freelancers skilled in photography can find diverse opportunities across various sectors. Sub-niches include:

- Product photography
- Drone photography
- Travel photography
- Event and portrait photography

This comprehensive list encompasses a wide range of niches and sub-niches that freelancers can explore based on their skills and interests, highlighting some of the most lucrative and emerging areas for freelancing.

2. Standout in Your Niche

"Chose the niche that you enjoy, where you can excel and stand a chance of becoming an acknowledged leader."- **Richard Koch.**

Understanding how to excel by aligning your career with your unique strengths and passions is critical to standing out. In *What You're Really Meant to Do: A Roadmap for Reaching Your Unique Potential* (HBR Press), Robert Steven Kaplan explains that standing out isn't about following the crowd—it's about discovering and leveraging what makes you distinctive.

Kaplan notes that many professionals, despite financial success, remain unfulfilled. This is because monetary rewards alone don't provide lasting satisfaction. People often chase roles that society deems prestigious, driven by external rewards like money, status, or titles. However, these extrinsic motivators rarely lead to true fulfillment.

To stand out in your niche, it's crucial to focus inward. Rather than pursuing "hot" jobs that may not suit your skills and interests, you must identify your strengths, weaknesses, and passions. Kaplan emphasizes that you own your career path, and the more you understand yourself, the better you can carve out a niche where you can truly shine.

Excelling in your niche is not a one-time achievement but a continuous process that requires self-assessment, learning from mentors and coaches, and adapting your skills to the changing demands of your field. Your strengths and weaknesses are not fixed; they evolve with the job at hand. To stand out, focus on building self-awareness, leveraging feedback from others, and investing in long-term skill development.

By understanding your intrinsic motivators and seeking roles that align with your unique potential, you can not only stand out in your niche but also find greater fulfillment and long-term success in your career. It's not just about finding a job, but about finding a role that allows you to fully utilize your strengths and passions.

Find Your Passion

"Marketing is really just about sharing your passion." — **Michael Hyatt.**

Many studies highlight a strong connection between passion and high performance in the careers of highly effective people. Those who believe in their mission and enjoy their work operate at a higher level, with a sense of purpose that drives success and fulfillment. But how do you find this passion and connect it to your professional life?

Connecting passion to work can be challenging. It involves making trade-offs, adjusting mental models, and reflecting on one's deepest desires. Passion is an emotional force and a critical factor in helping one push through challenges. When things get tough, passion often keeps one moving forward.

Exercises and mental models help students at the beginning of their careers identify and filter out options that don't resonate with their core values. For mid-career professionals, passion can fade as job requirements evolve or as they change personally. It is essential to look back at times when you were at your best—when you loved your work and received positive reinforcement for it.

Here are some thought-provoking questions and mental models that can help guide your journey of discovering or reigniting your passion:

1. **If you had one year left to live**, how would you spend it? What activities or career paths would you pursue that bring you joy and passion?

2. **If money were no object**, what job or career would you choose?

3. **If you were guaranteed success**, what career would you pursue without hesitation?

4. **What would you like to tell your children or grandchildren** about what you've accomplished in your career?

5. **If you were advising yourself as a third party**, what career path would you suggest for your future?

Balancing intrinsic motivators, such as passion, learning, and belonging, with extrinsic goals like money, status, and power allows you to mix passion with practicality. Finding the right combination of these elements will guide you toward a fulfilling and successful career. Passion is the key to unlocking your full potential, and it's critical in achieving a sense of purpose and accomplishment in life.

Process of Finding Your Passion

When it comes to *finding your passion* as a foundation for identifying a profitable niche, the key lies in discovering a balance between what excites you and what can serve others.

Following steps will help guide you toward uncovering your true passion:

1. **Reflect on Your Interests**: Start by listing things that genuinely interest you. These could be hobbies, skills, or topics you can discuss endlessly. Your passion often resides in activities that bring you joy and fulfillment. As you narrow your interests, ask yourself: "What would I love to do, even if I wasn't paid for it?"

2. **Explore Your Experiences**: Think back on your personal and professional journey. Identify moments where you felt the most alive, engaged, or accomplished. These experiences are often signals of where your passions lie. Brainstorm your current (or future) story for each interest.

3. **Connect Passion to Service**: Passion alone doesn't create a sustainable career path. You must also identify how your passion can solve

a problem or fulfill a need for others. Dig deeper into your chosen area and find a sub-niche where products, services, or solutions are already in demand.

4. **Infuse Personal Touch**: Add a personal touch to connect with your audience. Your passion is unique because it's yours—bring your authentic self to it. The more you share your story, the more you'll attract people who resonate with your message.

5. **Commit to Your Passion**: Have a commitment statement that solidifies your focus on turning passion into a purposeful and profitable venture. Affirm or keep this commitment visible in your workspace to remind yourself why you're pursuing this path.

By following these steps, you can find a passion that aligns with your strengths and interests while also being mindful of how it can serve others, making it a profitable niche.

Stress often stems from not finding passion in what you're doing. The moment you align your values with your work, that stress transforms into purpose-driven effort, fuelled by passion and a desire to achieve.

16 MBTI Business Owner Types:

You ever wondered how your personality shapes your approach to entrepreneurship? The Myers-Briggs Type Indicator (MBTI) offers valuable insights into how individuals prefer to work, make decisions, and interact with others. Understanding your MBTI personality type as an entrepreneur can help you identify your strengths and challenges, build a team that complements you, and create a business strategy that best suits your style.

We'll explore the 16 MBTI business owner types, helping you uncover the entrepreneurial traits that set you apart. Discover your entrepreneur type and how it can guide your business journey.

1. ESTP - The Bold CEO Entrepreneur

Passion: Action and Results

Driven by excitement and challenges, ESTP entrepreneurs thrive in fast-paced industries. They excel at making quick decisions and taking bold risks, making them ideal for roles that require dynamic leadership and direct action, such as in startups, tech, or sales-driven companies.

2. ENTP - The Visionary Innovator Entrepreneur

Passion: Exploration and Experimentation

ENTPs constantly generate new ideas and enjoy challenging the status quo. Their innovative spirit suits them for industries like tech development, creative agencies, or any business that values disruption and growth. They love building from scratch.

3. ESTJ - The Structured Executive Entrepreneur

Passion: Organization and Efficiency

Highly organized and focused on getting results, ESTJs are natural managers. They thrive in industries where structure, tradition, and clear hierarchy are valued, such as manufacturing, logistics, or any role that demands operational excellence.

4. ENTJ - The Charismatic Leader Entrepreneur

Passion: Ambition and Achievement

ENTJs are strategic and efficient, thriving in competitive environments. They are drawn to roles where they can lead large teams or make critical decisions, often excelling in corporate consulting, strategic management, or finance.

5. INTJ - The Quiet Strategist Entrepreneur

Passion: Innovation and Mastery

INTJs are long-term planners who love solving complex problems. They often excel in tech, engineering, or research-driven businesses, where they can methodically build and scale products or services precisely.

6. ISTJ - The Detail-Oriented Operator Entrepreneur

Passion: Reliability and Structure

ISTJs excel in managing well-organized, process-driven companies. They enjoy industries like law, finance, or construction, where attention to detail and adherence to rules are critical for long-term success.

7. ESFJ - The Caring Team Builder Entrepreneur

Passion: Service and Relationships

ESFJs excel in industries where they can support and lead teams through empathy and collaboration, such as in HR, event planning, or service-oriented businesses like hospitality or healthcare.

8. ESFP - The Adventurous Creator Entrepreneur

Passion: Fun and Creativity

ESFPs thrive in environments where they can work hands-on and see immediate results. They often succeed in creative fields like fashion, entertainment, or experiential marketing, where their energy and people skills can shine.

9. INFP - The Purpose-Driven Caregiver Entrepreneur

Passion: Meaning and Values

INFPs are deeply committed to causes they believe in. They excel in socially conscious businesses or creative endeavors, such as non-profits, arts organizations, or counseling services, where they can align their work with their values.

10. INFJ - The Visionary Advocate Entrepreneur

Passion: Vision and Impact

INFJs are idealists who want to change the world through their work. They excel in fields like coaching, consultancy, or writing, where they can combine their strong vision for the future with their ability to understand people deeply.

11. INTP - The Logical Problem Solver Entrepreneur

Passion: Intellectual Challenges and Solutions

INTPs love exploring new theories and systems, making them suited for tech startups, engineering firms, or R&D, where they can apply their logical and analytical skills to innovate and improve processes.

12. ISFP - The Artistic Creator Entrepreneur

Passion: Creativity and Aesthetics

ISFPs are hands-on creators with a strong sense of aesthetic and personal expression. They excel in creative industries like design, photography, or crafts, where their artistry can directly influence the business.

13. ISFJ - The Reliable Caregiver Entrepreneur

Passion: Support and Service

ISFJs enjoy roles where they can help others in a structured environment. They often thrive in caregiving businesses, such as health and wellness, education, or community services, where they can focus on improving the lives of others.

14. ISTP - The Resourceful Problem-Solver Entrepreneur

Passion: Hands-on Work and Problem Solving

ISTPs enjoy building and fixing things. They excel in trades or technical industries such as mechanics, carpentry, or any field that requires a practical, hands-on approach to solving problems.

15. ENFJ - The Inspiring Team Leader Entrepreneur

Passion: Leadership and Growth

ENFJs are natural coaches and motivators, often excelling in fields like education, leadership training, or public relations, where their ability to inspire and lead teams toward a common vision is crucial for success.

16. ENFP - The Charismatic Connector Entrepreneur

Passion: Ideas and Interaction

ENFPs are passionate and energetic. They thrive in industries where they can interact with others and bring new ideas to life. They often succeed in media, marketing, or entrepreneurial ventures that require constant innovation and collaboration.

This breakdown ties each MBTI type to an entrepreneurial style aligned with their key strengths and passions, helping to connect your personality with the right business path.

3. Create Value for Your Audience

"Focus on identifying your target audience, communicating an authentic message that they want and need, and projecting yourself as an "expert" within your niche."- **Kim Garst.**

Creating value for your audience is at the heart of any successful business. It's not just about the product or service you offer; it's about how well it solves a specific need for your target market. One of the most common reasons startups fails is that they don't take the necessary steps for an in-depth understanding of their audience. Building something your audience truly wants requires more than an idea—it takes insight, research, and genuine connection. Your audience is not just a market, but a vital part of your business's success.

The first step is finding a niche audience that resonates with you. Look for a group with similar preferences, values, and sensibilities. By focusing on a specific audience, you can tailor your message and offerings to meet their needs more effectively. Remember who your core audience is, and serve that niche with dedication.

To thrive in any niche, it is essential that one becomes an expert in their field. Conjointly, share valuable, actionable information with your niche audience, even taking it one step forward by providing free content to build trust. Referencing other trusted experts can further solidify your credibility. Your goal should be to create a harmonious relationship between your offer and your audience's needs.

In today's world, a niche doesn't have to mean small. With the global reach of the internet, a focused area of expertise can attract millions of potential customers. This potential should fuel your ambition and optimism. Finding your unique space or creating one, can lead to long-term success, as your value lies in your ability to serve your niche authentically and effectively.

Ultimately, success comes when you find the perfect balance within your niche—where you can offer something valuable, connect with your audience, and make a lasting impact.

Find Your Audience

To effectively find and build your niche audience, it's essential to blend research with strategic engagement. Follow these key steps:

1. **Identify their needs and pain points**: This step is about gathering data and showing your audience that you care about their specific problems and desires. Research what they are searching for, their frustrations, and unmet needs. Platforms like Google, Facebook groups, Quora, and other forums offer insights into the discussions and questions raised by your potential customers.

2. **Target them precisely**: Instead of casting a wide net, focus on a niche segment within your broader audience. This approach shows

that you value each individual within your audience and are willing to cater to their needs. This may involve analyzing demographic details such as age, gender, occupation, and geographical location, along with psychographics such as their interests, lifestyle, and values.

3. **Speak their language**: Use the terminology and tone that resonates with your audience. Tailoring your message to their unique needs shows that you understand them deeply. Whether through social media posts, blogs, or emails, customize your communication style to align with their preferences.

4. **Find them where they hang out**: Engage with your audience on platforms they actively use, such as specific social media sites, niche forums, or industry-specific blogs. Consider running ads, posting guest articles, or

participating in conversations in these spaces.

5. **Connect on a personal level**: Building a real connection with your niche audience is more impactful than just promoting your products or services. Share stories, testimonials, and authentic experiences that create trust and relatability. Personal connections strengthen your brand's long-term loyalty.

How to create Value for your Audience

In order to provide solutions, you must first be aware of the audience's pain points. Conduct keyword research using tools like Google Trends to explore what's trending in your niche. Simultaneously, researching competitors allows you to identify market gaps and refine your unique value proposition. Competitor analysis is critical to understanding the profitability of your niche.

Once you've identified your niche, testing its profitability is crucial. Run small experiments like ads directing users to a landing page to gauge interest, or use crowdfunding platforms like Kickstarter to validate your idea. These steps help ensure that your niche has enough demand before fully committing resources.

Finally, focus on establishing a solid foundation through ongoing market research and prioritizing refining your audience's needs. This focus on refining your audience's needs makes them feel prioritized and catered to. Engaging in competitor analysis will help you continually improve your positioning and maintain your audience's trust. By following these strategic steps, you'll find your niche audience and create a business that resonates with them on a deeper level, resulting in a loyal customer base and sustained growth.

How to Create an Effective Value Proposition

Defining a clear value proposition is one of the most critical elements of starting or scaling a business. This concise statement highlights why customers should choose your product or service over competitors. This statement forms the foundation of your brand's promise and sets you apart in a crowded market.

We'll explore the essential steps to craft a compelling value proposition:

1. **Identify Your Customer's Job to Be Done**

   Every successful value proposition begins by addressing a core need or problem your customers face. By applying Harvard Business School Professor Clayton Christensen's "jobs to be done" theory, you'll learn to view your product as an offering and a solution that customers' hire' to accomplish something. Understanding this deeper motivation is critical to positioning your brand effectively.

2. **Analyze What Differentiates Your Brand**

   What makes your product unique? Is it price, quality, convenience, or a social mission? By assessing the competition and pinpointing what sets your brand apart, you can clarify your product's specific benefits that are absent in others. For example, Warby Parker's affordable, stylish eyewear combined with a commitment to social good helped define its value proposition and captured the attention of consumers.

3. **Craft a Clear and Concise Statement**

   Once you understand the problem you're solving and what distinguishes your brand, it's time to put it into words. A strong value proposition should be simple yet powerful, typically no more than a few sentences. It should communicate what you offer, why it matters, and how it's different—creating an instant connection with potential customers.

4. **Test and Refine Your Proposition**

   To ensure your value proposition resonates with your target audience, test it with real people. Share it with those unfamiliar with your business to see if they understand the core message. If there's any confusion, adjust it to ensure clarity and impact.

By mastering the art of crafting a value proposition, you'll create a strong foundation for your brand that helps convert leads into loyal customers and enables you to pitch confidently to investors and partners. This clear, concise message becomes a powerful tool in building long-term success and market differentiation for your business.

A profitable niche is one where your offerings are highly sought after, and people are willing to pay for the value you provide. Choosing the right niche requires careful consideration of several factors to balance market demand, competition, and your ability to serve and grow within the niche effectively.

Selecting the Most Profitable Niches for Businesses

Identifying profitable niches is a critical step for entrepreneurs and small business owners seeking to carve out a successful space in the market. Here's a structured approach to selecting the most profitable niches:

1. **Market Demand and Size**

   Research the potential customer base and their demand for your product or service. A niche with a large and growing market is generally more profitable.

2. **Competition Level**

   Assess the number and strength of competitors in the niche. Niches with moderate competition can indicate profitability, while overly saturated markets may present challenges.

3. **Profit Margins**

Consider niches with higher profit margins. Factor in production, marketing, and distribution costs to ensure the niche is financially viable.

4. **Passion and Expertise**

Aligning the niche with your interests and knowledge can improve business decisions. Passion can sustain motivation, especially during challenging times.

5. **Trends and Sustainability**

Look for niches with lasting appeal rather than fleeting trends. Sustainability can indicate long-term profitability.

6. **Market Accessibility**

Consider how easily you can reach and serve the target market. Niches with accessible market channels tend to be more profitable.

7. **Regulatory Environment**

Understand the regulations and compliance requirements within the niche. Highly regulated sectors may pose barriers to entry and incur additional costs.

8. **Scalability**

   Choose niches that offer room for growth and expansion. The ability to scale can significantly impact long-term profitability.

9. **Innovation Potential**

   Niche markets that allow for innovation can provide a competitive edge. The potential for product or service evolution can drive profitability.

10. **Online Potential**

    Assess the niche's viability for online sales and marketing. A strong online presence can broaden your market reach and enhance profitability.

11. **Supply Chain Stability**

    Reliable and efficient supply chains can bolster profitability. Evaluate the ease of sourcing materials and the stability of your suppliers.

10 Most Profitable Niches and Subniches

Health, **Wealth**, and **Relationships** niches continue to dominate the market, reflecting consistent consumer interest and profitability. These niches allow content creators, businesses, and entrepreneurs to thrive. Here's a breakdown of the most profitable niches and sub-niches, along with emerging trends that offer high potential:

1. Health and Wellness

- **Nutrition:** Diet plans, healthy recipes, and nutritional advice.

- **Exercise:** Workout routines, fitness challenges, and exercise equipment reviews.

- **Mental Health:** Mindfulness, stress management, and mental health awareness.

- **Holistic Health:** Alternative medicine, natural remedies, and holistic practices.

- **Supplements:** Reviews and recommendations of vitamins, minerals, and herbal supplements.

2. Personal Finance and Investing

- **Budgeting:** Tips and tools for managing personal finances.
- **Debt Management:** Strategies to pay off debt and improve credit scores.
- **Investing Basics:** Guides on stocks, bonds, and mutual funds.
- **FIRE Movement:** Stories and strategies from those pursuing early retirement.
- **Real Estate Investing:** Tips on buying, selling, and managing properties.

3. Relationships

- **Dating & Marriage Counseling:** Guidance for romantic relationships.
- **Life Coaching:** Support for personal and professional growth.

- **Parenting & Homeschooling:** Tips for raising children and alternative education.
- **Workplace Networking & Communication:** Strategies for professional relationships.
- **Divorce Recovery:** Support and advice for navigating separation.

4. Digital Marketing

- **SEO:** Helping businesses rank higher on search engines.
- **Content Marketing:** Creating valuable content to attract and retain customers.
- **Social Media Marketing:** Engaging audiences on Instagram, Facebook, and LinkedIn platforms.
- **Email Marketing:** Building relationships and driving sales through email campaigns.
- **PPC Advertising:** Managing paid advertising campaigns on Google, Bing, and social media platforms.

5. Technology and AI

- **Tech Trends:** Latest innovations and future predictions.
- **Software Reviews:** In-depth reviews of new and popular software.
- **AI Applications:** Practical uses of AI in various industries.
- **VR and AR:** Virtual and augmented reality technologies.
- **Web3 and Blockchain:** Decentralized Internet and cryptocurrency trends.

6. Blogging and Making Money Online

- **Building a Blog:** Step-by-step guides on starting a blog.
- **Finding Your Audience:** Strategies to attract and retain readers.
- **Monetization Models:** Ways to make money from blogging, including ads, sponsored posts, and affiliate marketing.
- **Side Hustles:** Ideas and tips for earning extra income online.

7. Sustainable and Ethical Products

- **Eco-friendly:** Products that minimize environmental impact.

- **Biodegradable:** Items that break down naturally and safely.

- **Reusable:** Alternatives to single-use products.

- **Ethical Sourcing:** Ensuring products are made with fair labor practices.

8. Travel and Adventure

- **Travel Guides:** Destination guides and travel tips.

- **Budget Travel:** Affordable travel options and hacks.

- **Luxury Travel:** High-end travel experiences and accommodations.

- **Travel Gear:** Reviews of travel accessories and equipment.

9. Parenting and Childcare

- **Pregnancy:** Tips and advice for expecting parents.
- **Baby Care:** Guides on newborn care and development.
- **Parenting Styles:** Different approaches to raising children.
- **Family Activities:** Ideas for family bonding and fun.
- **Product Reviews:** Reviews of baby and parenting products.

10. Recipes and Food

- **Specific Cuisines:** Recipes from various cultures.
- **Meal Planning:** Tips for efficient and healthy meal prep.
- **Food Photography:** Techniques for capturing mouth-watering photos.
- **Food Trends:** Latest trends in the culinary world.

Whether your focus is on Health, Wealth, or Relationships, these top niches and their sub-niches offer immense potential for profitability. By understanding these trends and tailoring your content or business offerings to these profitable areas, you can tap into consumer demands and build a thriving, long-term venture.

Want to get our book for free?

Discover the 16 different personality types with MBTI. Each of us has unique talents that make our personality shine. Want to dive into the deeper psychology of your type, explore your special cognitive functions, and find your path to personal growth? Scan the QR code below to grab your free copy of the Personality Handbook now.

About Clear Career Inclusive

At Clear Career Inclusive, we understand that every career journey is unique. That's why our books are packed with practical tips, real-world strategies, and inclusive advice designed to support diverse career paths and experiences. Our easy-to-understand guidance is crafted to fit seamlessly into your busy life.

Our mission is to provide you with clear, comprehensive, and actionable career advice that helps you grow both professionally and personally. We believe that career success isn't just about working harder—it's about working smarter with the right insights and strategies.

Join us on this journey to career success. With Clear Career Inclusive, every step you take is a step towards a more inclusive, brighter, and successful future. **Reach out to us at:** contact@clearcareer.in

May We Ask for a Review?

Thank you for reading this book. We would appreciate it if you could share your thoughts and review it.

Direct Review Link

We sincerely welcome your input to help us deliver an even better book shortly. If you have any suggestions or would like to share your thoughts directly, please feel free to reach out to us at:

contact@clearcareer.in

Your support is instrumental in our journey. It will help us reach more readers and we deeply appreciate it. Thank you for being a part of our success. We look forward to reading your review, and don't hesitate to contact us if you need any clarifications.

Warm regards,

Clear Career Inclusive

www.clearcareer.in

Acknowledgement

We extend our deepest gratitude to the readers of this book for your time, reviews, and invaluable feedback. Your support and insights have been crucial in shaping this work.

Thanks to everyone who contributed their experiences, encouragement, and assistance throughout this journey.

Thank you.

References

1. NICHE | English meaning - Cambridge Dictionary
2. How To Choose Your Niche: 8-Step Formula + 120 Niche Ideas (createandgo.com)
3. The Most In-Demand Freelance Niches in 2024 (millo.co)
4. MBTI Business & Entrepreneur Personality Types [16 Most Common] (thryv.com)
5. The Step-By-Step Guide to Finding Your Niche and Target Market | Entrepreneur
6. How To Identify And Build A Niche Target Audience For Marketing (forbes.com)
7. How to Create an Effective Value Proposition | HBS Online
8. The 21 Most Profitable Niches to Get Into (smallbiztrends.com)
9. Top 13 Trending Niches in 2024: What's Hot and Profitable? - The Niche Guru

10. Most Profitable Niche 2024: Top 10 Lucrative Trends (skup.net)

11. NICHE NAVIGATOR: HOW TO FIND A PROFITABLE NICHE IN 1 HOUR - Miles Beckler

12. What You Are Really Meant to Do: A Roadmap for Reaching Your Unique Potential (HBR Press), Robert Steven Kaplan

TEST LINKS

1. www.16personalities.com – For the MBTI test

2. www.truity.com – For the Enneagram test

3. www.truity.com – Free Big Five Personality test

4. www.truity.com – DISC Assessment Free Personality Test for Business

5. www.truity.com – Holland Code Job Aptitude Test

Made in the USA
Las Vegas, NV
07 January 2025

15938222R00046